JAVA Programming for Beginners

The Simple Guide to Learning JAVA Programming fast!

Table Of Contents

Introduction

I want to thank you and congratulate you for downloading the book, *"JAVA Programming for Beginners"*.

Java is everywhere, and programmers who've used it are often split into to factions: ones who swear by it and ones who curse its existence. Java can seem clunky and inefficient for people who haven't realized its full potential, since a lot of advanced Java books tend to get overly technical.

Programming isn't just jamming a bunch of commands to a system hoping to get a valid response; it's a systematic way of teaching the dumbest student in the world: the computer. What a lot of people get wrong in trying to learn Java is reading dry reference books and trying to memorize the commands.

Whether you're looking for a relaxing way to advance your career in Java, or simply want to use Java as a gateway to the world of programming, this book will teach you not only the syntax of Java, but also the best way to master Java even after you've finished this book.

The first few sections of this book shall be relatively simple, in order to acclimate you to programming and Java, but several sections down the road you'll find yourself immersed with complex concepts. However, Java is a huge language with a lot of different commands, so expect that this book will leave out sections for you to learn by yourself. When you're done with this book, you should be well acquainted with Java and equipped with the tools and mindset to develop Java applications.

Thanks again for downloading this book, I hope you enjoy it!

Chapter 1:
Java Demystified

In this chapter, you will become acquainted with Java. Some common misconceptions about Java will also be addressed so that in succeeding chapters you will more or less have an idea about what Java can do, how to use it, when to use it and when not to use it.

By the end of this chapter, you should have a strong overview of object-oriented programming while getting a glimpse of the Java programming language. In short, this chapter will serve as your foundation in both programming and Java concepts. No programming exercises shall be done in this chapter, but you're free to try some of the codes used in this chapter if your machine can already compile and run Java.

An Overview of Programming

Humans have finally found a way to create something that would obey their commands without as much as a whine or a whimper. The consequence, however, is a rather dumb machine that needs special instructions via a special language.

People new to the world of programming often ask, "Can't we make machines that can understand human language?" The problem with human language is that it contains so many complexities such that even syntactically correct sentences could still be misunderstood. It also becomes exponentially harder to formulate sentences when you try to give complicated instructions. Lastly, many words present in the English language evolve with time, such that some words become unnecessary while some have their meanings changed because of the way people use them. So while current technology may allow the creation of a machine that can understand a bit of human language, it would require complicated algorithms and massive computing power that's not yet widespread.

Computers are used practically everywhere because of their unmatched precision and accuracy in performing complex calculations. Unfortunately, as computer users want more of the thinking done by the computers, programmers have to put in extra effort in teaching the computers how to think more like a human being.

Why learn to program?

Imagine asking a friend to draw you a scene you've seen in a dream. When he shows you his drawing, you aren't quite satisfied so you go to another friend asking the same favor. To your disappointment, he doesn't even come close to the scenery you've seen, either. Eventually you realize that most of the artists you know cannot produce the scene you had in mind, so you decide to learn how to draw. You know that drawing is a complicated endeavor, but you also know that it gives you a chance to do things exactly your way. This is what programming allows you to do. Sometimes you just really want to have features that most programmers don't bother putting in their products. You might also have an idea of a program that could make a group of people's lives easier and would like to implement it yourself. In short, programming allows you to improve upon what's already present, or create something completely new.

What is Java?

Java is one of the most common programming languages available. Most Universities teaching computer science teach this language in the first semester to introduce programming to the new students. Because it was built with the improvement of C++ in mind, Java syntax is much closer to human language and is generally much easier to use.

Because of Java's "Write Once, Run Anywhere" philosophy, Java programs can be run practically anywhere with a Java runtime environment installed. Programmers can use Java to develop almost all kinds of programs from browser games to database handlers, which makes it an ideal programming language to start with.

Java vs. C

There's an ongoing debate as to which language should be taught in introductory programming courses. While Python is making its way into the debate, C and Java still dominate most computer science courses due to their widespread applications and huge demands for programmers who know these languages.

So what are the differences between Java and C, apart from C being a much older language? In this section, we shall distinguish between the two dominant programming languages and in the process teach you more about the nature of the Java programming language. Here are the major points that separate Java from C:

1. Language Type

Aside from the different keywords and syntax, the way the language works is also different; Java is an object-oriented programming language whereas C is a function-oriented programming language. As their names suggest, object-oriented programming is focused on being able to add new objects to your code easily, while function-oriented programming is focused on being able to add new functions or operations to your code easily. Don't worry if this isn't too clear to you now; as we go deeper into the heart of Java you'll learn why this distinction is important.

2. Portability

Portability, in a nutshell, means being able to send your code to your friend's computer and still have it running the same way as it would if it ran on your computer. Processors are the brains of every computer, some wired differently than the others. As mentioned before, Java was created with portability in mind, so both the source and compiled code can run on machines with different "brains," simply because Java provides an interpreter that helps different processors understand the same code. If you're using C, on the other hand, you'd have to make sure that the code you're typing won't use certain functions that other operating systems may not have. Also, since C does not provide an interpreter, you need to recompile your code for different types of processors for your programs to work properly.

3. Memory management and manipulation

Many computer viruses are created using C because of its power to manipulate memory. Memory addresses can be manipulated and could be used to exploit security holes in an operating system. Because of C's power to directly access memory, it's endowed with the power to manipulate hardware. This kind of power, however, is not without its cons; beginners could easily forget to release memory that they've been using, causing some computers to lock up and freeze. This is especially problematic if a program with memory leaks has already made its way into other people's computers. Java, on the other hand, remembers to release memory once you're done using it and is less likely to crash a system. It also provides mechanisms to try catching possible memory problems so your program can continue running even after a serious problem.

4. Usage in the real world

C is often used in places where speed and power are needed. Since C does not have an interpreter, it's much faster than Java. Java, on the other hand, is used in places where portability is important, and since today most modern machines run different processors, a lot of people prefer Java especially in programs that don't require massive amounts of computing power.

Basics of Object-Oriented Programming

Now that you have a nice bird's eye view of Java, let's take a closer look at the concepts of object-oriented programming, namely:

- A. Objects

- B. Classes

- C. Inheritance

- D. Interfaces

- E. Packages

Now let's go through each one thoroughly:

- A. Objects – The concept of objects is what Java is firmly grounded on. In real-world terms, objects could be anything sitting on your desk, being cooked in your kitchen, being cleaned at the laundry, etc. Now focus on a tiny segment of your home and examine the objects in that place. How would you describe the objects in that segment? In most cases you may say that the objects are clean or dirty, working or defective, etc. You may also describe the objects according to what they do, like dishwashers cleaning dishes, toasters toasting toast, etc. Just like objects in the real world, objects in Object-Oriented Programming are also characterized by their *states* and *behavior*. In the world of Java, an object's state is stored in *fields*, while an object's behavior is stored in *methods*.

Imagine if manufacturers allowed people to give very specific commands to appliances like microwave ovens, such that one could change the security setting to allow it to operate even with the door wide open. That would cause a lot of accidents and mishaps, which is why manufacturers only allow people to operate their machines through a bunch of predefined commands. This translates to the world of Java as *data encapsulation*, wherein objects can only communicate with each other using prescribed methods.

B. Classes – If all appliances were created by hand, imagine how long it would take manufacturers to make them and how expensive they would be! In the world of Java, classes are like blueprints; they contain what an object's state could be and what it can do. For example, if we need to create a bunch of colored pens, we just need a class that contains what the pen could do, what its color is, etc. Then these attributes would be followed when the pens are manufactured. The manufactured pens would then be called an *instance of the Pen class*.

Here's a sample code of a possible implementation of a pen:

```
class Pen {

    int color = 0;

    boolean writing = false;

    boolean empty = false;


    void changeColor(int newValue) {

        color = newValue;

    }

    void changeWriting(int newValue) {

        writing = newValue;

    }

    void changeEmpty(int newValue) {

        empty = newValue;

    }

    void printStatus() {

        System.out.println("Color:"      +
color + " Writing:" + writing + "Empty?:"
+ empty);

    }

}
```

In this code, the pen has three variables: color, writing, and empty. What these variables contain will basically tell you what color the pen has, whether it's currently being used to write something or not, and whether it's empty or not. The methods available allow you to change the color of the pen, toggle the "writing" and "empty" states, and print the current state of the pen.

Notice that the code presented above does not really do anything; we've just created a blueprint of a pen and nothing more. Here's a code that makes use of the class we've just created (think of this as a factory that follows the given blueprint):

```
class PenFactory {

    public    static    void    main(String[]
args) {

    //Create two new pens!

    Pen pen1 = new Pen();

    Pen pen2 = new Pen();

    //Do       stuff       allowed       by       the
"manufacturer"

    pen1.changeColor(9);

    pen2.changeWriting(false);

    pen1.printStatus();

    }

}
```

C. Inheritance – In the real world, pens could have different shapes, ink types, brands, etc. The previous code can just be adjusted accordingly, but what if we were to include pens that could record video and audio and therefore must include states called "recordingVideo" and "recordingAudio"? Pens with no such functions would have no use for such states. Fortunately, instead of having to create a completely different class for these high-tech pens, the object-oriented programming paradigm allows classes to *inherit* states and behavior from other classes. This means that high-tech pens and low-tech pens could just get states and behavior from the Pen *superclass* while having special states and behavior for their own classes. Here's a sample code of the high-tech pen class:

```
class HighTechPen extends Pen {

    boolean recordingVideo = false;

    boolean recordingAudio = false;


    void toggleRecordingVideo() {

        recordingVideo = !recordingVideo;

    }

    void toggleRecordingAudio() {

        recordingAudio = !recordingAudio;

    }

}
```

```
    void printStatus() {

        System.out.println("Color:"      +
color + " Writing:" + writing + "Empty?:"
+    empty    "Recording    video?"    +
recordingVideo + "Recording audio?" +
recordingAudio);

    }

}
```

Notice how in this code we no longer had to add color and other fields already present in the pen superclass. When you *extend* a class, you *inherit* all the methods and fields it already has. Programmers don't like to have to repeat writing the same code. Just make sure to document the methods and fields present in your superclass properly so that people who want to create subclasses from your superclass will know what methods and fields are at their disposal.

D. Interface – Real world objects often have a prescribed set of commands you can do with them, for example, some showers allow you to choose the temperature from freezing cold to scorching hot with a turn of the knob. This knob is the interface between you and the shower, allowing you to control its state. In the world of Java, an interface is a collection of methods. One might think of this as a brochure of an object. Here's what the Pen interface would look like:

```
interface Pen {

    void changeColor(int newValue);

    void changeWriting(int newValue);

    void changeEmpty(int newValue);

    void printStatus();

}
```

Now here's what an *implementation* of this interface would look like with a brand of pen called *StarPen*:

```
class StarPen implements Pen {

    int color = 0;

    boolean writing = false;

    boolean empty = false;

    public void changeColor(int newValue)
{

        color = newValue;

    }

    public      void      changeWriting(int
newValue) {

        writing = newValue;

    }

    public void changeEmpty(int newValue)
```

```
{
        empty = newValue;

    }

    public void printStatus() {

            System.out.println("Color:"      +
color + " Writing:" + writing + "Empty?:"
+ empty);

    }

}
```

You might be wondering how this differs from the first Pen class we've created. When you create a class that implements an interface, you basically make a promise that you're going to provide the method bodies present in the interface. In real life, you'd expect all faucets to provide a way for you to control when water is dispensed, so when someone creates a blueprint of a faucet it's understood that he would need to provide specific details on how the faucet dispenses water, whether it pulls water from a nearby lake or from an electronic pump.

E. Packages – Packages basically combines classes and interfaces that are similar to keep them organized. For example, classes that contain methods that would allow you to print stuff are found in java.awt.print. This allows programmers to find whatever commands they're looking for without having to dig through thousands of lines of code. To see all of the available packages in Java, simply go to https://docs.oracle.com/javase/8/docs/api/index.html and explore its contents.

Conclusion

In this chapter, you've been given a brief overview of object-oriented programming and Java so that the succeeding chapters make much more sense. Think of this chapter as a quick dip into the world of Java and object-oriented programming. The next chapter will take you on a test drive as you set-up your computer for Java and then writing, compiling, and running your first Java program!

Chapter 2:
Your First Java Program

Before going straight into coding, let's talk about how the Java platform works so that you'll have a general idea what happens beneath the abstractions. After that we're going to talk about getting your computer ready for Java so that you run into minimal problems later. After equipping you with a Java platform primer and the necessary tools to write, compile, and run Java, you get to create your first Java program!

How the Java Platform works

The Java platform lets you write and compile programs via the Application Programming Interface (API) and the Java Virtual Machine (JVM).

Imagine getting a trained dog. You've been trying to get him to do tricks like "sit" or "play dead", but he just stares at you looking confused. As it turns out your trainer had trained your dog to respond to different terminologies. What do you do? In most cases, you'd ask for a list of commands your trainer has trained you dog to respond to. Java APIs work similarly, in a sense that they provide you with a list of tricks that Java already knows. In your first Java application, you're going to use a Java API to output a line of text to your screen. Without that Java API, you're going to have to use a more complicated bunch of commands instead of just a line of code in order to display a simple line of text.

Now imagine going on a world tour just for the heck of it. You find out, however, that with your current itinerary you'll need to learn 20 languages, because a lot of the countries you're planning to visit don't know English. Learning 20 languages can take a very long time, so you decide bring an electronic translator with you. This makes it possible to understand people and be understood in foreign, non-English-speaking countries. In almost the same way, Java Virtual Machine allows your code to be understood by different machines running different operating systems powered by different processors.

Getting your computer ready for Java

Before writing, compiling, and running Java applications, you'll have to install the Java Platform on your machine. You can download the version appropriate for your system free of charge from www.oracle.com. The installation is rather straightforward so there'll be no need for a walkthrough; just follow the installation instructions and you'll be fine.

The Java Platform is really all you'll need to compile and run Java applications, together with any text editors in order to write code. While one can opt to use the built-in text editors of operating systems, they're not particularly helpful when it comes to debugging your code or highlighting certain parts of it. With that in mind, you can use advanced text editors made for programming. Here are some of the best text editors for writing Java code:

- VIM – This isn't a text editor beginners tend to like, but once you get used to programming in VIM you'll be able to write code a lot faster.

- Notepad++ - A lot of programmers like using Notepad++ because it's free and it was created with programmers in mind so you can be sure that it supports the most common programming languages like Java and C. It also runs pretty fast compared to other text editors.

- Atom – Atom is a relatively new text editor specifically created for programming. A lot of people do complain, however, that it's not as lightweight as Notepad++. Atom supports more programming languages, including web development frameworks.

If you just want a no-fuss text editor with a very small learning curve, opt for Notepad++. If you want a text editor with more features and customization options, opt for Atom. If you want a text editor that lets you create code really fast and don't mind the steep learning curve, opt for VIM.

The provided text editors should be enough for the code snippets and exercises written in this book, but if you want an even easier and more guided way to code Java, you can opt for Eclipse, which is an Integrated Development Environment (IDE). The reason why IDEs are popular is because they let you "pause" your code and find bugs in your program while it's running. IDEs are often equipped with a wide range of diagnostic and testing tools, not to mention code completion to make the programmer's life a lot easier. With this description you might be wondering why not all people use IDEs; while IDEs make programming oftentimes a lot easier, they tend to use a lot of memory. Also, for programming experts they tend to get slowed down by IDEs because of their heavy reliance on graphical user interface.

In the end, the choice is yours. Whether you want to program with trainer wheels (Eclipse) or straight onto the mountain bike (VIM) or somewhere in-between, the important thing is that you know what exactly you're coding and how to debug it.

Creating your first program

In order to create your first program, simply copy this segment of code into your text editor or IDE:

```
//My First Program!

class FirstProgram {

    public static void main (String[] args) {

        System.out.println("Hi there!");

    }

}
```

Save this code as FirstProgram.java. Remember that the name of the files should be the name of the main function as well! Also, note that Java considers "FirstProgram" different from "firstprogram" so be particular about lowercase and uppercase letters!

Compiling your first program

If you're using Linux or Mac OSX, simply run the terminal and type in the following command:

```
javac FirstProgram.java
```

If you're using Windows, you'll have to do these additional steps:

1. Find "Advanced system settings" in the control panel

2. Click "Environmental Variables"

3. Click "System Variables"

4. Put the bin directory of the Java platform you've just installed in the beginning of the PATH variable. The bin directory should look more or less like: C:\Program Files\Java\jdk1.6.0\bin.

Don't worry; you'll only have to do this once. After doing these four steps, open command prompt and type in the same "javac" command indicated earlier.

If you're using Eclipse or any other IDEs, just press the "run" button and you're good to go.

Running your first program

After compiling the program, you can now run your simple program on any machines that have a Java Platform installed. If you've used text editors to create your program, simply type the following command to run your first program:

```
java FirstProgram
```

If you're using Eclipse or other IDEs, the run button would have automatically compiled and run the program for you.

That's it! You have just made your first Java program! Congratulations! It does feel like a lot of work just to produce a boring line of text, doesn't it? Don't worry; in the next chapters we'll be able to create much more powerful programs. It only looks complicated because it's new, but with further practice and good coding standards, you could be as good in coding as you are with speaking in your native language!

Good programming practices

When you think about it, anyone can learn Java, or C, or any other programming language. So how come there aren't many programmers around? Why is there a predicted shortage of more than 50% of qualified programmers? What separates good programmers from bad programmers is not necessarily the level of knowledge of Java syntax; rather, it's the programming practices. Here's a list of what good programmers do that separates them from bad programmers:

1. Good programmers place comments in their code so that other people reading it can understand what they're doing. Sure, you can create codes without comments if it's a simple hello world program, but when you create large scale applications that require sharing your code to other people, having comments in your code could save hours or days of work trying to figure out what your code does. If you want to comment only a single line, use this format:

```
//This is a comment
```

Notice the double slashes – anything you type in that line after the double slashes will not be compiled and run. It's also good for "turning off" lines of code! Try putting a double slash before the "System.out...." line and see what happens.

If you want to comment multiple lines, use this format:

21

```
/*

This is still a comment!

*/
```

Notice the /* and */ that encloses the comment. This allows you to comment more than one line and "turn off" a whole segment of code as well.

The last type of comment syntax is probably one of the most important: Doc Comments. Here's the format:

```
/**

This is a comment that javadoc will use to
generate API documentation.

*/
```

This type of comment is important because it allows you to create documentation for whatever you're writing. Documentation basically tells people what your code does and how to use it. Large-scale applications make use of documentation heavily because code gets passed around quite often.

Experienced programmers know the pain of having to interpret somebody's code for hours, days, or even weeks just because they were too lazy to type in a few lines of code explaining how it functions and how it's used. Don't be that programmer; make it a habit to comment on your code whenever you feel that other people may have a hard time understanding what you wrote.

2. Good programmers use Github or any other file versioning system. The days of emailing and copying code from flash drives are over; file versioning systems are now becoming more popular because they allow people to work on the same piece of code without recklessly overwriting each other's work. If you don't know what Github is, visit the site, create an account, and go through their tutorials. Remember that some programming companies hire people depending on how active they are on Github – that's how important it is to the programming community.

3. Good programmers, well, program a lot! Technically this isn't a programming practice, but remember that programming is about learning how to explain complex, real life problems to a machine that thinks in ones and zeroes. This takes years of practice to master and cannot be accomplished by passively reading textbooks. Follow along the exercises in this book and try your best to become an active reader by asking questions and verifying facts being presented to you, and you'll be several steps closer to being a Java master.

Recap

In this chapter, you've learned four major concepts:

1. The basics of the Java Platform

2. How to get your machine ready to write, compile and run Java programs

3. How to write, compile, and run your first Java program

4. Tips to become a good programmer

Don't worry if you feel that you haven't accomplished much yet; you've experienced what a lot of programmers call "set-up time". Set-up time is a period wherein programmers learn the syntax of a programming language while installing stuff on their machines in order to make their programs compile and run. In the next chapter we're going to take a closer look at what's happening inside Java programs in order to prevent confusion when it comes to debugging.

Chapter 3:
More Than Just Hellos

What comes after "Hi There"?

After making your first hello world Java program, you might have asked yourself, "What's next?"

In order to make programs that can actually do useful stuff, we're going to have a very thorough discourse about how to get your programs to:

A. Store information

B. Do some operations on certain types of data

C. Follow certain protocols when conditions are met

This set of information will allow you to create very simple programs that can do more useful things like calculate the sum of two numbers, get the average of a given group of numbers, etc.

A. Storing information

Back in Chapter 1, notice that the Pen class had these lines of code that were able to store states:

```
int color = 0;

boolean writing = false;

boolean empty = false;
```

Here are some of the questions you might have asked yourself after seeing this code segment:

a. What is `int` or `boolean` for? Are there any keywords that function similarly?

b. Am I free to name my variables any way I want?

c. Do I always have to give my variables an initial value? What happens if I don't?

To help you understand the code presented, here's a brief summary of the code snippet:

- `int` is the *data type* of the *variable* `color`.

- `boolean` is the *data type* of the *variables* `writing` and `empty`.

- The *initial value* of `color` is 0

- The *initial value* of `writing` and `empty` are both `false`.

Now let these statements percolate in your mind as you're given a more thorough explanation about data types, variables, and initial values.

Variables – You'll rarely create programs that don't require the user to input data into the program. Variables let your program remember what the user has just typed so that you can process them later.

There are four kinds of variables in Java:

a. Local Variables – drawings are a way to project one's fantasies and dreams into a two-dimensional reality. In a way, local variables are like drawings because they only exist in whatever medium they're created. Here's a rough Java code snippet to make things clearer:

```
{

    char dream = 'U';

}

System.out.println(dream);
```

This code would cause Java to complain because outside those brackets, `dream` does not exist. In future discussions regarding classes and functions you'll be using brackets quite a lot, so remember to create variables in the appropriate places so you avoid referring to stuff that don't exist.

b. Parameters – parameters are almost like local variables in a sense that they only exist inside specific brackets. A rather rough analogy would be an arcade game; when you insert a token, that token could be represented in the arcade as a character that you control. While the token you inserted exists outside the arcade game, the character you play with does not. Here's a complete Java code for you to try:

```
class test {
    public    static    void    main(String[]
args) {
        System.out.println("Game
Character Representation: " + game(65));
        System.out.println("Actual Game
Character: " + character);
    }

    public static char game(int token) {
        char character = (char)token;
        return character;
}
```

The parameter in this code is `token`, while the local variable is `character`. Can you figure out which line in this code won't work and why it won't work?

c. Instance Variables – if you remember our analogy with pens and classes, we had a variable named `color`. Every manufactured pen - or in terms of Java – every instance of the Pen class will have its own variable named `color` as well, because it really doesn't make sense to have only one color for all the pens being manufactured. Instance variables are basically variables that have unique values for the instances of classes that they correspond to.

d. Class Variables – when you add the keyword `static` when you declare a variable, it immediately becomes a class variable. Unlike instance variables, when you change values inside instance variables the change will cascade to all the instances of whatever class uses that variable.

Now that you've gotten a thorough explanation regarding variables, let's talk about the rules and accepted conventions when it comes to naming your variables. Take note that some experienced people do break conventions when they absolutely need to, but as a beginner, you're going to want to stick to the accepted conventions. As for the rules, however, your code won't even compile if you break even one rule, so at all costs, make sure you follow the rules of naming variables.

a. Conventions

    i.   Always start the variable name with a letter.

    ii.   As much as possible, *dnt* create *vrble nmes lyk dis* – the compiler will accept this type of naming, but most programmers will not appreciate it and might even find it cryptic.

    iii.   If your variable name consists of only one word, resist the urge to capitalize the first letter.

    iv.   If your variable contains a value that won't change throughout the program, all of its letters should be in uppercase. If it happens to have more than one word, separate the words using "_".

b. Rules

    i.   The variable name can only start with either a letter or the symbols "$" or "_".

    ii.   Variable names can't have spaces in-between; if you want to create variable names that contain several words, use CamelCase or snake_case instead.

iii. Variable names are case-sensitive; a variable named "pie" will be treated as a completely different variable from "PiE".

iv. You can't use any of these *reserved keywords* as your variable name:

A	D	G	P	T
abstract	default	goto	package	this
assert	do	I	private	throw
B	double	if	protected	throws
boolean	E	implements	public	transient
break	else	import	R	try
byte	enum	instanceof	return	V
C	extends	int	S	void
case	F	interface	short	volatile
catch	final	L	static	W
char	finally	long	strictfp	while
class	float	N	super	
const	for	new	switch	
continue		native	synchronized	

Now that we've explored the types of variables and proper naming conventions, let's now talk about data types.

Data Types – From the name itself, data types tell you what type of information the data contains.

Recalling the Java code snippet that allows you to store data:

```
int color = 0;

boolean writing = false;

boolean empty = false;
```

In this code, `int` or `boolean` are what Java calls Primitive Data Types. All variables have data types so that computers know how much space to give them and what type of operations can be done on them. Let's expound further what primitive data types are and what other primitive data types are available for you to use:

Primitive Data Types – Primitive data types are data types that Java has already defined for you. This means that you can't use them as names for variables, classes, etc. There are only eight primitive data types defined in Java:

- boolean – boolean data types can only store true or false values and therefore has a very small size of 1 bit.

- byte – byte data types can store integers with a size of only 8 bits.

- short – short data types can also store integers with a larger size of 16 bits

- char – char can store Unicode characters, which would mean one letter/number/symbol, with a size of 16 bits.

- int – int is the most commonly used data type because it can store integers with the standard size of 32 bits – enough to represent most of the integers you'd be using in standard programs.

- long – long is used when a program needs to store a really huge number that int can no longer store. With a size of 64 bits, it has twice the space that int has.

- float – float is used when you need to store numbers with decimal points. Like int it also has 32 bits of allocated space.

- double – double is used when float can no longer accommodate the size of a number with a decimal point. Like long it also has 64 bits of allocated space.

What's special about Java is that there's a special support for strings coming from the java.lang.String class. This means that you can easily create strings by typing a line of code like:

```
String sentence = "Hello world!";
```

Remember though that String is not considered a primitive data type, but since its usage is somewhat similar anyway you might as well use it as such.

Sanity Check

Now that you have a stronger grasp of data types and variables, we shall explore the idea of creating a collection of data: arrays. At this point, you may want to go back and skim this chapter once again from the beginning up to this text if you're not yet quite confident with the concepts of variables and data types since the next section assumes that you've fully absorbed the previous information given to you. Now is also a good time to take a break to let the concepts completely seep into your mind. If you're done, let's proceed.

Arrays – an array is basically a container that has a bunch of data of the same type. In real life, this would be similar to shelves in a supermarket; items on a single shelf are often of the same type, and the sizes of the shelves do not change after they have been manufactured. Let's discuss arrays a bit more to give you a better look at how they work.

Here's an example of an array declaration in Java:

```
int list[] = {1,2,3,4,5};
```

Each number inside the bracket is called an element. You can access these elements by referring to the variable name and the index of that element. For example, if you want to access the element "3" inside the list array, you'll need this expression:

```
list[2]
```

A lot of people make the mistake of counting from one when using arrays; in programming, counting always starts at zero so when you try to get the index of "3", which is two places away from "1", you'll have to use this correspondence:

```
Array: {1,2,3,4,5}

Index:  0,1,2,3,4
```

Here's a full sample code you could try:

```
class test {
    public static void main(String[] args) {
        // this line of code tells the
compiler that numbers will be an array of int.
        int[] numbers;

        // this line of code tells the
compiler that the numbers variable will need
five spaces to store five ints.
        numbers = new int[5];

        // these lines of code assign values
to specified indexes of the numbers array.
        numbers[0] = 1;
        numbers[1] = 2;
        numbers[2] = 3;
        numbers[3] = 4;
        numbers[4] = 5;


        System.out.println("The value at index
0 of the numbers array is: "
                        + numbers[0]);
        System.out.println("The value at index
1 of the numbers array is: "
                        + numbers[1]);
        System.out.println("The value at index
2 of the numbers array is: "
                        + numbers[2]);
        System.out.println("The value at index
3 of the numbers array is:"
                        + numbers[3]);
        System.out.println("The value at index
```

```
4 of the numbers array is: "
                        + numbers[4]);


    }
}
```

B. Doing some operations on certain types of data

We've had very thorough discussions about variables and their power to store information, but in the first place the point of storing information is to be able to do something interesting with it and have something useful come out as a result. *Operators* allow you to do specific operations on a couple of variables or values. That being said, we're going to have a rather thorough discourse about operators before we go into larger scale code like statements and blocks.

Before going into the specifics of operators and their usage, it's a good idea to know about which operators have the highest precedence. Back in grade school, you've probably been taught the MDAS rule, which states that you should do multiplication and division operations before doing addition and subtraction operations. In Java, you also have to learn rules similar to this one because a simple switch in the order of operations could mess up your answer. The list provided below gives the order of precedence of the operators, from highest to lowest.

Operators	Description
`variable++` or `variable--`	Gives you the current value inside the variable before adding or subtracting one from that value
`++variable` or `--`	Adds or subtracts one from

`variable`	the current value inside the variable and then gives that value to you
`*`, `/`, or `%`	Allows you to get the product, the quotient, or the remainder-if-divided (modulo) of two or more numbers
+ or −	Allows you to get either the sum or the difference of two or more numbers, but if you're using these on a single number then you're basically turning that number positive or negative.
<, >, <=, >=, or `instanceof`	Every operator here except the `instanceof` compares two numbers and tells you if the first number is less than, greater than, less than or equal to, or greater than or equal to the second number. The `instanceof` operator tells you if an object is an instance of a specified class.
== or ! =	Tells you if two numbers are equal (==) or if two numbers are unequal (! =)
`&&`	Lets you combine operations and tells the compiler that all of the operations combined must return `true`

			Also lets you combine operations, but this one tells the compiler that at least one of the operations must return `true`
? and :	This tandem called the ternary operator allows you to create a rather concise if-else statement.
=, +=, -=, *=, /=, or %=	The = sign allows you to assign a value to a variable, while the rest of the operators here allow you to add, subtract, multiply, divide, or modulo a number on the right side of the operator to the variable on the left side of the operator.

There are other operators like bitwise and shift operators, but we won't discuss them since they're rarely used. We shall talk a bit more thoroughly about the operators given and have some sample codes for you to try.

First off, let's talk about the most basic operators you're most likely already familiar with: arithmetic operators. The arithmetic operators in Java consist of:

a. `*` - Multiplies two numbers

b. `/` - Divides two numbers

c. `%` - Gets the module of two numbers

d. + - Adds two numbers

e. - - Subtracts two numbers

Here's an example of a Java program that uses these arithmetic operators:

```
class test {

    public static void main (String[] args) {

        //multiplies 5 and 2 and outputs the
product, 10, to the screen.
        int product = 5 * 2;
        System.out.println("5 * 2 = " +
product);

        //multiplies the product, 10, with 2
and outputs it to the screen.
        product *= 2;
        System.out.println("product *= 2 = " +
product);

        //divides 5 and 2 and outputs the
quotient, 2.5, to the screen.
        double quotient1 = 5 / 2;
        System.out.println("5 / 2 = " +
quotient1);
        //Whoops! What happened here? Is 5
divided by 2 really 2.0?

        //Let's try adding .0 to five and two:
        double quotient2 = 5.0 / 2.0;
        System.out.println("5 / 2 = " +
quotient2);
        //That's more like it! Always remember
to add a decimal point to at least one of the
numbers you're using so that Java doesn't
treat your numbers like integers.
```

```
        //divides the quotient, 2.5, by 2.0.
Can you guess what happens when you remove the
.0 from 2.0? While it might seem logical to
get a wrong answer like 1, quotient2 is
already a double, you don't need to have the
.0 at the end of 2. It's still good practice,
though.
        quotient2 /= 2.0;
        System.out.println("5  /  2  =  "  +
quotient2);

        //gets the remainder when you divide 5
by 2. you should get 1.
        int modulo = 5 % 2;
        System.out.println("5  %  2  =  "  +
modulo);

        //gets the sum of 5 and 2, which is 7,
and outputs it to the screen.
        int sum = 5 + 2;
        System.out.println("5 + 2 = " + sum);

        //gets the difference of 5 and 2,
which is 3, and outputs it to the screen.
        int difference = 5 - 2;
        System.out.println("5  -  2  =  "  +
difference);


    }
}
```

Play around with the code and see what you get! Don't forget
to place code comments to help you remember what you're
trying to do and what outputs you expect.

Notice how we've been using the + operator outside the quotation marks quite a lot. This is because the + operator doesn't only help you add numbers, but it also allows you to combine strings! Try going back to the code you just ran and play around with the + operator.

Now let's talk about incrementing or decrementing variables. Explicitly telling the compiler to add simple constants like five and two is easy, but postfix and prefix operators may be a bit confusing for a lot of people. Here's a sample code using postfix and prefix operators in different scenarios. Before compiling and running this code, try to guess what their outputs would be and compare it to the actual output.

```
class test {
    public static void main(String[] args){
        int i = 1;
        i++;
        System.out.println("Getting the value
of i AFTER using i++, with i=1 initially : " +
i);

        i=1;
        ++i;
        System.out.println("Getting the value
of i AFTER using ++i, with i=1 initially : " +
i);

        i=1;
        System.out.println("Getting the value
of i WHILE using ++i, with i=1 initially : " +
++i);

        System.out.println("Getting the same i
AFTER ++i  : " + i);

        i=1;
        System.out.println("Getting the value
```

```
of i WHILE using i++, with i=1 initially : " +
i++);

        System.out.println("Getting the same i
AFTER i++ : " + i);
    }
}
```

Now that you can add, subtract, multiply, divide, modulo, increment, and decrement numbers, and concatenate strings in Java, it's time to look into operators that let you compare values: equality and relational operators. Since they only compare values, they don't need to modify the operands. Also, they can only return either true or false depending on the result of the comparison. The equality and relational operators consist of:

== - checks if two values are the same

!= - checks if two values are not the same

> - checks if the value on the left is greater than the value on the right

>= - checks if the value on the left is greater than or equal to the value on the right

< - checks if the value on the left is less than the value on the right

<= - checks if the value on the left is less than or equal to the value on the right

Here's another Java sample code that uses equality and relational operators. Again, don't just compile and run the code without taking intelligent guesses about what the outputs will be. Try to infer what the results would be first and then compare it to the actual results.

```
class test {

    public static void main(String[] args){
        int number1 = 1;
        int number2 = 2;
        int number3 = 2;

        System.out.println("Is    number1    ==
number2?");
        if(number1 == number2)
            System.out.println("yes");
        else
          System.out.println("no");

        System.out.println("Is    number1    !=
number2?");
        if(number1 != number2)
          System.out.println("yes");
        else
          System.out.println("no");

        System.out.println("Is    number1    >
number2?");
        if(number1 > number2)
          System.out.println("yes");
        else
          System.out.println("no");

        System.out.println("Is    number1    >=
number2");
        if(number1 >= number2)
          System.out.println("yes");
        else
          System.out.println("no");
```

```java
        System.out.println("Is     number2     >
number3?");
        if(number2 > number3)
          System.out.println("yes");
        else
          System.out.println("no");

        System.out.println("Is     number2     >=
number3");
        if(number2 >= number3)
          System.out.println("yes");
        else
          System.out.println("no");

        System.out.println("Is     number1     <
number2?");
        if(number1 < number2)
          System.out.println("yes");
        else
          System.out.println("no");

        System.out.println("Is     number1     <=
number2");
        if(number1 <= number2)
          System.out.println("yes");
        else
          System.out.println("no");

        System.out.println("Is     number2     <
number3?");
        if(number2 < number3)
          System.out.println("yes");
        else
          System.out.println("no");

        System.out.println("Is     number2     <=
number3");
        if(number2 <= number3)
          System.out.println("yes");
```

```
            else
                System.out.println("no");
        }
    }
}
```

Real world comparisons aren't this simple, however. In most cases, you'll be dealing with multiple comparisons. In Java, we can accomplish this simply by combining equality and relational operators using conditional operators. The conditional operators consist of:

&& - returns true if both conditions are satisfied

|| - returns true if at least one condition is satisfied

Here's a simple Java code that shows how conditional operators may be used:

```
class test {

    public static void main(String[] args){
        int number1 = 1;
        int number2 = 2;
        int number3 = 2;

        System.out.println("Is    it    true    that
number1 == number 2 AND number2 == number3?");
        if((number1 == number2) && (number2 ==
number3))
            System.out.println("Yep");
        else
            System.out.println("Nope");

        System.out.println("Is    it    true    that
number1 == number 2 OR number2 == number3?");
        if((number1 == number2) || (number2 ==
```

```
number3))
            System.out.println("Yep");
        else
            System.out.println("Nope");
    }
}
```

Basically, this code tells us that && just means AND, and ||
means OR. Now let's go into the ternary operator, ? and :.

When programming newbies come across a ternary operator
they're often intimidated, but it's actually just a more compact
way of writing an if-else statement. In this next sample Java
code we just convert the previous code's if-else statements into
ternary operators:

```
class test {

    public static void main(String[] args){
        int number1 = 1;
        int number2 = 2;
        int number3 = 2;

        System.out.println("Is  it  true  that
number1 == number 2 AND number2 == number3?");
        System.out.println(((number1         ==
number2)   &&   (number2   ==   number3))   ?
"Yep":"Nope");

        System.out.println("Is  it  true  that
number1 == number 2 OR number2 == number3?");
        System.out.println(((number1         ==
number2)   ||   (number2   ==   number3))   ?
"Yep":"Nope");
    }
}
```

Notice how this makes the code shorter, but it could impair your ability to skim through a code quickly since this operator tends to look cryptic. Just remember that while it may act like an if-else statement, you can't put functions that don't return values as the result if the statement before the ? operator is satisfied.

The last comparison operator is the `instanceof` operator. It's quite different from the operators we've been using because it's used not on primitive data types, but on objects. The `instanceof` operator basically tells you if an object is an instance of a class or a subclass. Here's a sample Java code that uses `instanceof`:

```
class test {
    public static void main(String[] args) {

        Pen object1 = new Pen();
        HighTechPen      object2     =      new
HighTechPen();

        System.out.println("Object1          an
instance of Pen? " + ((object1 instanceof Pen)
? "yes" : "no"));
        System.out.println("Object1          an
instance   of   HighTechPen?   "   +   ((object1
instanceof HighTechPen) ? "yes" : "no"));
        System.out.println("Object1          an
instance   of   AdvancedFeatures?   "   +   ((object1
instanceof AdvancedFeatures) ? "yes" : "no"));

        System.out.println("Object2          an
instance of Pen? " + ((object2 instanceof Pen)
? "yes" : "no"));
        System.out.println("Object2          an
instance   of   HighTechPen?   "   +   ((object2
instanceof HighTechPen) ? "yes" : "no"));
```

```
        System.out.println("Object2        an
instance of AdvancedFeatures? " + ((object2
instanceof AdvancedFeatures) ? "yes" : "no"));
    }
}

class Pen {}
class HighTechPen extends Pen implements
AdvancedFeatures {}
interface AdvancedFeatures {}
```

C. Following certain protocols when conditions are met

You've already gotten a glimpse of this when you've come across if-else statements. Code that lets your program do certain tasks with certain conditions are called *Control flow statements*. In a nutshell, they give your program the power to decide. There are three types of control flow statements we shall discuss:

a. Statements that allow your program to make decisions

b. Statements that allow your program to do stuff repeatedly for a precise number of times

c. Statements that allow your program to pause, continue, or exit

Sanity Check

Now is a great time to take a break. The rest of the material in this book will have less exhaustive treatment so that you'll have a chance to explore and experiment with codes yourself. A great trait to have as a programmer is the innate sense of adventure and curiosity, so don't be afraid to change bits of codes and search for additional references if you're lost. *Stackoverflow* is a great website to search for solutions for common problems in programming. Take a quick skim through the entire book up to this point and review the codes that were provided, as the next section will force you to think critically and search for additional resources as you deem necessary.

Decision-making statements

There are two types of decision-making statements:

1. *if-then* and *if-then-else* statements – this is probably the most familiar to you since we've used them quite a lot in the previous sections. Here are the basic templates for *if-then* and *if-then-else* statements:

```
//if-then

if(condition)

{

    //do whatever is inside this block if condition is fulfilled

}
//if-then-else

if(condition)

{

    //do whatever is inside this block if condition is fulfilled
```

```
}

else

{

    //do whatever is inside this block if
condition is not fulfilled

}

//if-then-else with multiple else-ifs

if(condition1)

{

  // do whatever is inside this block if
condition1 is fulfilled

}

else if(condition2)

{

  // do whatever is inside this block if
condition1 is not fulfilled but condition2 is
fulfilled

}

else if (condition3)

{

    //do whatever is inside this block if
condition1 and condition2 are not fulfilled
but condition3 is fulfilled
```

```
}

else

{

    //do whatever is inside this block if none
of the conditions are fulfilled

}
```

2. *switch* statement – the *switch* statement is quite similar to the *if-then* and *if-then-else* statements, the only difference being a bit more limited because it only works on primitive data types such as byte, short, char, int, with the exception of the String class and enum types. Here's the basic template for a switch statement:

```
switch(variable)

{

    case [can be a number, a character, a
string, or an enum]:

        //do whatever is inside this block if
first case is fulfilled

    break;

    case [can be a number, a character, a
string, or an enum]:

        //do whatever is inside this block if
first case is not fulfilled but the second
case is
```

```
        break;

    case [can be a number, a character, a
string, or an enum]:

        //do whatever is inside this block if
first and second cases are not fulfilled but
the third case is

    break;

    default:

        //do whatever is inside this block if
none of the cases are fulfilled

    break;

}
```

Looping statements

Looping statements allow your program to do something repeatedly for a fixed number of times. There are two types of looping statements:

1. while and do-while statements

while statements are like if-then statements, but this time if the condition specified holds true, then whatever is inside the block of code will be executed again and again until the condition no longer holds true. Of course, this means that you'll have to do something that eventually makes the conditions false within the block of code; otherwise you're going to experience what people call an endless loop. Here are the basic templates for the while and do-while statement:

```
//template for while

while(condition, e.g., x < 10)

{

    //code here will be executed again and
again if the condition still holds true


    //there should be something that
eventually breaks the condition, e.g., x++;

}

//template for do-while

do

{

    //code here will be executed again and
again if the condition still holds true


    //there should be something that
eventually breaks the condition, e.g., x++;


} while(condition);
```

The difference between the while and do-while statements is that the do-while statement is guaranteed to execute the code inside at least once, while the while statement has a chance of not executing the code inside at all.

2. for statements

for statements are more compact than while statements and is best used in codes that have rather short conditions for iteration. Here's the basic template for the for statement:

```
for(initialize    variable,    e.g.,    x   =   0;
condition,   e.g.,   x  <  10;   iterate   variable,
e.g., x++)

{

    //do whatever is inside this block as long
as the condition specified still holds

}
```

Branching statements

There are three commands used for branching:

1. *break* – this command allows you to break outside a loop or a labeled statement. Here's a template for its usage:

```
for(initialize    variable,    e.g.,    x   =   0;
condition,   e.g.,   x  <  10;   iterate   variable,
e.g., x++)

{

    //do whatever is inside this block as long
as the condition specified still holds

    //this next segment of code breaks you out
of the for loop as long as condition1 is met.
```

```
if(condition1)

{

    break;

}

}
```

2. *continue* – *continue* allows you to go to the next iteration of a loop. Here's a template for its usage:

```
for(initialize    variable,    e.g.,    x    =    0;
condition,  e.g.,  x < 10;  iterate  variable,
e.g., x++)

{

//this next segment of code allows you to skip
whatever comes after the if-statement and go
right into the next iteration of the loop if
condition1 is met.

    if(condition1)

    {

        continue;

    }

    //do whatever is inside this block as long
as the condition specified still holds

}
```

3. return – this statement simply lets you exit the current method you're in. you can either return a value or not, depending on whether or not the method says it needs a value returned. Here are templates for its usage:

```
//returning with a value

if (condition)

{

    return variable;

}

//returning without a value

if (condition)

{

    return;

}
```

Congratulations! You now know how to store data, do stuff to it, and let your program make decisions. You should now be able to create simple programs, like a program that adds two numbers, and other operations. In the final chapter we shall talk about the essential Java classes every Java programmer should know. That chapter should wrap-up everything you've learned so far and give you the power to learn new Java classes all by yourself.

Chapter 4:
Into the heart of Java

You've trudged through the basics and the nuances of the Java language. You've explored data types, variables, operators, conditions, etc. Now that you can "talk the talk", it's time to "walk the walk" by learning essential Java classes that you'll most likely be using. The knowledge you've obtained from the previous chapters shall be put to the test.

After this chapter, you will be well equipped with the most important concepts you need to write efficient and bug-free Java programs. Here's a quick overview of the topics to be tackled:

A. Exceptions and Exception Handling– dealing with stuff that might prevent your program from running smoothly

B. Multithreading – making your programs run lots of tasks at the same time

C. I/O

Sanity Check

Now is a great time to take a break if you've been immersed in this book for more than an hour. This section will only teach the basics of what most Java developers consider essential, so a lot of extra research and thinking will come from you. Take a few minutes to relax and then take a really fast skim of the previous chapter before you dive straight into the next lesson.

A. Exceptions and Exception Handling

Back in the old days of procedural programming, even the simplest errors could crash a program and cause hours of work to go to waste. Fortunately, Java allows programmers to use *exceptions* to try to *catch* errors before they break the program.

An *exception* is simply shorthand for "exceptional event", which means that when a program is prevented from doing what it's supposed to do, then that means that an *exceptional event* is happening. When this happens, the method where the event has occurred creates an *exception object*, which contains a detailed description about the error that happened. This handoff of errors is called *throwing an exception*.

It isn't enough to know what the error is; the runtime system will try to find ways to get the program back to its normal state. It'll look for a block of code called an *exception handler* until it finds one that can handle the error. If it can't find the appropriate exception handler for the error, the program then crashes.

Before trying to catch and fix exceptions, let's talk about the three types of exceptions first:

a. Checked exceptions – checked exceptions are usually errors that the user causes, for example, by trying to open a file that does not exist.

b. Runtime exceptions – runtime exceptions are usually errors that the programmer probably caused.

c. Errors – the cause of these may either be the error of the user or the programmer. Usually there is very little one can do about errors in the context of exception handling since they're not even considered exceptions.

How to catch exceptions

`try` and `catch` are a formidable duo used to catch exceptions. You normally enclose a code that could possibly generate an exception with the `try` and `catch` combo. Here's a template:

```
try

{

    //Code that might generate exception

} catch(Exception_name e)

{

    //Code that attempts to resolve the
problem

}
```

Now here's a sample Java code that you can try:

```
import java.io.*;
public class test{

    public static void main(String args[]){
        int a[] = new int[3];
        //Accessing a nonexistent element with
try+catch
        try{
        System.out.println("Attempting     to
access element 3 :" + a[3]);
        }catch(ArrayIndexOutOfBoundsException
```

```
err){
        System.out.println("Exception   thrown
:" + err);
      }
    System.out.println("Program        still
running!");
      //Accessing    a    nonexistent    element
without try+catch
      System.out.println("Access element three
:" + a[3]);
    System.out.println("Program        still
running!");
    }
}
```

In a C program, accessing an element that doesn't exist would've immediately crashed the program. In this code, however, notice that trying to access the fourth element of an array that only has three elements caused the program to throw an exception but still manage to continue to the next line of code. After that though, the next segment of code tries to also access the fourth element of a size-3 array, but without the try+catch combo. Notice how this segment crashes the program and does not let the last println function get executed.

For methods that don't handle checked exceptions, simply use the *throw* + *throws* combo. These keywords would be better understood by the following sample code:

```
public class test{

    public static void main(String args[]){
        int a[] = new int[3];
```

```
        try
        {
         accessElementOfArray(3,a);
        } catch(ArrayIndexOutOfBoundsException
e) {
            System.out.println("Exception:  " +
e + " caught!");
        }
      System.out.println("Program        still
running!");


    }


   public static void accessElementOfArray(int
index,         int[]         array)         throws
ArrayIndexOutOfBoundsException
    {
      // Method implementation
       System.out.println("Attempting         to
access    element    "    +    index    +":    "    +
array[index]);
      throw                              new
ArrayIndexOutOfBoundsException();
    }
}
```

This code merely demonstrates what throws + throw does, so remember that if you're catching an exception using try + catch you don't need throws + throw.

Lastly, remember that try + catch will be your most used weapon in dealing with exceptions. Just remember to only catch exceptions that you intend to deal with. If you catch an exception and not do anything your program may either freeze or crash.

B. Multithreading and Concurrency

Computers, for the most part, are better multitaskers than humans are. Java takes advantage of this fact by allowing the creation of multithreaded programs. This means that you can have your program do several tasks at once, especially if you have a multicore CPU.

Threads have their own life cycle, almost like cellular organisms. Here are the different stages of their life cycle:

a. New – when a thread is born, it spends its life waiting for the program to give it purpose.

b. Runnable – when a thread is finally started, it becomes runnable. This is the stage where the thread is currently fulfilling its purpose.

c. Waiting – when a thread is in the waiting state, its life is put on hold. This usually happens when another task or thread has a higher priority and needs to be run urgently.

d. Timed waiting – this is basically the same as waiting, but with a specified time limit for that pause. This means that after the time limit expires, the thread can go back to its normal business.

e. Terminated – when a thread is terminated it either means that it has completed its purpose or it was killed prematurely.

How to create a thread

There are two ways of creating a thread:

1. By implementing the Runnable Interface – should be used if you plan to run your class as a thread

2. By extending the Thread Class – believed to provide less flexibility but more simplicity when it comes to handling multiple threads

Now let's go through each one more thoroughly.

Implementing the Runnable Interface

Remember our talk about interfaces as a promise to implement specified methods? The Runnable interface requires you to implement a `run()` method. It should look something like this:

```
public void run() {

//Your code here

}
```

After creating implementing the run() method you'll have to instantiate a *Thread* object using the following code:

```
Thread(threadObject, threadName);
```

Lastly, you'll have to call the *start()* method to get your thread up and running.

Here's a whole Java code for you to experiment with:

```java
public class test implements Runnable {

    public void run() {
        System.out.println("Finally    using    a
thread!");
    }

    public static void main(String args[]) {
        (new Thread(new test())).start();
    }

}
```

Extending the Thread Class

Since the Thread class already implements the Runnable interface, extending the Thread class will allow you to create threads as well, but with less flexibility. Here's another Java code you can use to experiment with this concept:

```java
public class test extends Thread {

    public void run() {
        System.out.println("Finally    using    a
thread!");
    }

    public static void main(String args[]) {
        (new test()).start();
    }

}
```

Can you spot the difference between this code and the code used to implement the Runnable interface?

We won't get into the nitty-gritty details of multithreading, as that would be beyond the scope of this book. Let's move on to the last part of the Java essentials:

C. I/O

Notice how we've only dealt with code that had no user input yet. All programs you create will more or less have user input, so we'll deal with the most common way to obtain input from the user: using the *Scanner Class*. In order to do that, we first need to instantiate an object from the scanner class, and then use the available methods to get input, such as:

1. nextInt – to get an integer

2. nextFloat – to get a float

3. nextLine - to get a string

Here's a sample code that uses the Scanner Class and its methods:

```
import java.util.Scanner;

class test
{
    public static void main(String args[])
    {
        int a;
        float b;
        String s;

        Scanner          userInput          =          new
Scanner(System.in);
```

```
        System.out.println("What's   your   name?
");
        s = userInput.nextLine();
        System.out.println("Hello, "+s);

        System.out.println("Can  you  give  me  an
integer?");
        a = userInput.nextInt();
        System.out.println("You've given: "+a);

        System.out.println(s + ",  can  you  give
me a float this time?");
        b = userInput.nextFloat();
        System.out.println("You've given: "+b);
    }
}
```

There are other available methods to get input from other devices as well, but this one is the most commonly used and also the most simple.

That's it!

Congratulations! You've made it through the first half of the Java learning process. The rest of the learning process takes place outside this book and from the people you work or code with, the problems you run into, the open source projects you'll hopefully be contributing too, and the abundant internet resources regarding Java programming. By now you should be able to create simple programs from the concepts you've learned, but being able to create fancy programs with beautiful interfaces, accessing files, and other advanced functions will require further research and more hours of coding and studying. I hope that this final chapter gave you a glimpse of the possibilities that Java offers, and it inspired you to develop innovative Java applications.

Conclusion

Thank you again for downloading this book!

I hope this book was able to help you learn more about Java!

Java is an interesting language; it can be simple for those who need it to be simple, and complex for those who need it to be complex. This book contains jam-packed information about java told in a less serious manner so that you can absorb the concepts quickly without dying from boredom due to the dryness of content most textbooks offer.

As the overused saying goes, programming is a way of life – just as people who are good at solving real life problems have the potential to be great programmers, programmers who practice programming are bound to be great problem-solvers in real life as well. I hope that the concepts and exercises in this book made you into a better problem solver and helped you see both the world of Java and the real world differently.

The next step is to put the strategies provided into use, and start using Java!

Finally, if you enjoyed this book, please take the time to share your thoughts and post a review on Amazon. It'd be greatly appreciated!

Thank you and good luck!

www.ingramcontent.com/pod-product-compliance
Lightning Source LLC
LaVergne TN
LVHW050149060326
832904LV00003B/74